The Countertop Book

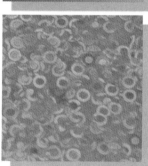

Mary Anne Piccirillo

Schiffer Publishing Ltd®

4880 Lower Valley Road · Atglen, PA · 19310

Other Schiffer Books on Related Subjects

Cast-in-Place Concrete Countertops. Tom Ralston. ISBN: 9780764329494. $39.95
Custom Kitchens: 50 Designs to Satisfy Your Appetite. Melissa Cardona & Nathaniel Wolfgang-Price. ISBN: 0764323962. $29.95
Glass Tile Inspirations for Kitchens and Baths. Patricia Hart McMillan & Katharine Kaye McMillan, PhD. ISBN: 0764325094. $19.95
Making Concrete Countertops with Buddy Rhodes: Advanced Techniques. Buddy Rhodes & Susan Andrews. ISBN: 9780764330148. $39.99

Schiffer Books are available at special discounts for bulk purchases for sales promotions or premiums. Special editions, including personalized covers, corporate imprints, and excerpts can be created in large quantities for special needs. For more information contact the publisher:

Published by Schiffer Publishing Ltd.
4880 Lower Valley Road
Atglen, PA 19310
Phone: (610) 593-1777; Fax: (610) 593-2002
E-mail: Info@schifferbooks.com

For the largest selection of fine reference books on this and related subjects, please visit our web site at **www.schifferbooks.com**
We are always looking for people to write books on new and related subjects. If you have an idea for a book please contact us at the above address.

This book may be purchased from the publisher.
Include $5.00 for shipping.
Please try your bookstore first.
You may write for a free catalog.

In Europe, Schiffer books are distributed by
Bushwood Books
6 Marksbury Ave.
Kew Gardens
Surrey TW9 4JF England
Phone: 44 (0) 20 8392 8585; Fax: 44 (0) 20 8392 9876
E-mail: info@bushwoodbooks.co.uk
Website: www.bushwoodbooks.co.uk

Disclaimer: The information provided in this book is based on consumer experience, industry standards, and averages. Consult the manufacturer for specific care instructions.

Title page image courtesy of ThinkGlass.

Copyright © 2010 by Mary Anne Piccirillo
Library of Congress Control Number: 2009932599

All rights reserved. No part of this work may be reproduced or used in any form or by any means—graphic, electronic, or mechanical, including photocopying or information storage and retrieval systems—without written permission from the publisher.
The scanning, uploading and distribution of this book or any part thereof via the Internet or via any other means without the permission of the publisher is illegal and punishable by law. Please purchase only authorized editions and do not participate in or encourage the electronic piracy of copyrighted materials.
"Schiffer," "Schiffer Publishing Ltd. & Design," and the "Design of pen and ink well" are registered trademarks of Schiffer Publishing Ltd.

Designed by RoS
Type set in Browallia New/Aldine 721 BT

ISBN: 978-0-7643-3392-7
Printed in China

Contents

Acknowledgments_____ 4

Foreword_____ 5

Glass_____ 6

Concrete_____ 26

Repurposed Materials_____ 42

Engineered Stone_____ 54

Extreme Engineered Stone_____ 84

Wood_____ 92

Soapstone and Slate_____ 102

Granite and Marble_____ 108

Metal_____ 118

Ceramic Tile_____ 126

Laminate_____ 132

Solid Surface_____ 142

Edge Profiles_____ 154

Resources_____ 159

Dedication

For the person who taught me to appreciate and understand beauty and who always had the ability to find it in everyone and everything – my mom. And, to my dad who gave us the time, love, and ability to enjoy that beauty.

Acknowledgments

If it weren't for Al Pirro, my fiancé, this book would never have been completed. He pushed and nagged and pushed some more to keep the words flowing. I should also mention that our first renovation together as a couple was new countertops for his house. We survived and they're beautiful. We chose granite; its foundation is as solid as his.

Also, thank you to the all of the Public Relations, Marketing, and Communications professionals who made wonderful images and information available. All of the resource companies listed in the back of the book are lucky to have such dedicated men and women representing them. To everyone who had to send their materials repeatedly because the computer gremlins were attacking the files, thank you for your patience and persistence.

A special shout out to two of the best interior decorators I've had the privilege to learn from, Linda Webb and Bob Hogg of Classic Quarters in Lancaster, Pennsylvania. They have let me tag along to photo shoots, installations, site visits, planning sessions – and dinner – more times than I can count. Please consider consulting them:

Linda Webb and Bob Hogg
Classic Quarters
Lancaster, PA
(717) 392-4843

To Tina Skinner at Schiffer Publishing – thank you for the opportunity.

Foreword

Countertops have a huge impact on the design of your kitchen. They reflect how you use your kitchen, how you view your kitchen, and what your kitchen says about your personality and style. They are the design element that unifies the cabinetry, flooring, hardware, appliances and lighting.

There are surfaces for every lifestyle, personality, and function with design capabilities that are limited only to one's imagination and pocketbook. Manufacturers and designers are reaching outside of conventional thought to develop unique materials and looks.

Some of the newest and developing looks incorporate glass, concrete, or semi-precious gemstones. Though they may have been on the market for some time, they are becoming more widely used and accepted thanks to evolving technology, design flexibility, and, in some instances, lower costs. Features like fiber optics embedded into concrete, back lighting semi-precious gemstones, and unusual texture and color in glass are also catching designers' attention.

Of course materials like laminates, solid surfaces, and engineered stone that have been around for a while are also evolving through new colors, patterns, textures, and manufacturing techniques. In fact, it's difficult to distinguish some of the manufactured materials from their natural stone counterparts!

Environmental conscientiousness is playing a huge role in emerging materials. Most countertop manufacturers are becoming greener by either adhering to eco-friendly practices or offering products that contain some type of recycled or repurposed material. Don't be surprised to see surfacing made from pre-consumer toilets, money, cardboard, or beer bottles that are really beautiful.

With all of these innovative materials available, it's a great time to be in the market for countertops. But, before shopping for countertops, do some homework in the following areas: personal preferences, budget, functionality, and materials.

Personal preferences – what appeals to you? Take a good look at what makes up your style and personality: the type and color of clothing and jewelry you wear: patterns, trendy, traditional, casual; the type of perfume you wear: exotic or earthy; where you shop: high-end department stores, boutiques, discount stores.

Budget – how much money is available? Now is the time to decide how much you really have to spend on your countertop. A clear understanding of your financial allotment will help keep you focused when you visit showrooms. Ask yourself how important the countertop is to your design. If you are looking primarily at resale, you may want to spend a little more in an effort to bump up value. Perhaps this is a renovation and countertops are the biggest change to the room and will require the lion's share of your budget.

Functionality – how will the surfaces be used? Observe how the kitchen is used: is it the heart of the home where the family members spend most of their time; are "foodies" constantly preparing gourmet meals; is reheating the main activity in the room; or is it strictly a utilitarian space?

Materials – which ones meet your needs? Now that you have an idea of your style, how much you have to spend, and how the surface will be used, start researching the materials. Look at the range of colors, patterns and textures available. Consider the level of care and maintenance each requires. Compare durability and repairability. And, of course, compare costs – including sub-surface preparation, materials, delivery, and installation.

The most important factor in finding the right countertop for your space is to enjoy the process. Take the time to better understand your household, goals, and style. Your home is a reflection of you – if you're happy, it will show.

GLASS

GLASS has probably the most distinctive look of all of the countertop materials available. The surface can be smooth or textured by sandblasting, melting, shattering, etching, or grooving. Its natural green tint is beautiful, but it can be tinted with translucent or opaque coloring either by adding color to the glass, applying it to the back, or laying it over another material. For more drama, lighting can be added around the perimeter or the entire countertop can be lit. Glass countertops can be manufactured in just about any thickness.

About the Material

Glass countertops are generally made of cast tempered glass. It is extremely durable and can withstand a fairly high weight, about 300lbs in some cases. The material is non-porous, making it one of the most hygienic surfaces available.

What's Good About It

- Distinctive designs and texturing.
- High degree of customization available.
- Almost impossible to stain.
- Can withstand high heat.
- Easy care and maintenance.
- Non-porous: no cross contamination.
- Suitable for Kosher kitchens.

What To Be Aware Of

- Scratches in some situations but texturing and creative underlayment materials can aid in camouflaging them.
- Can be a budget breaker.
- There is a small possibility of cracking or breaking if a heavy object is dropped on it.

Care | Cost

Care
- Use window cleaner or a solution of water and vinegar and a clean, soft cloth.

Average Cost
- $150 and up per square foot, installed.

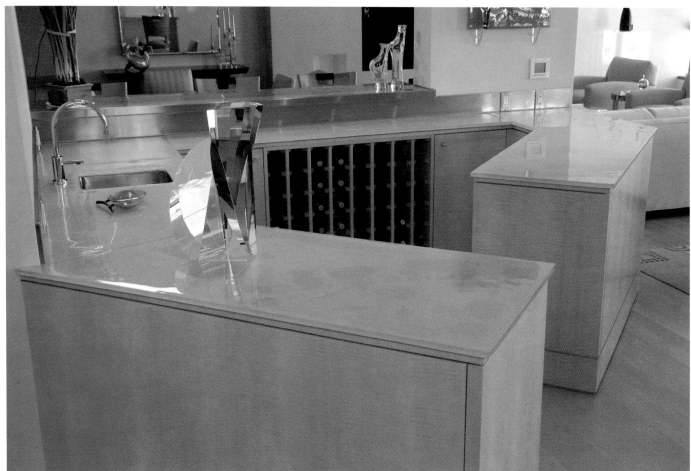

◄ ▲ A unique masterpiece of colorful infusion on the glass countertop completes the WOW factor of this very sophisticated kitchen. *Design by Michel Mailhot. Courtesy of ThinkGlass.*

◄ ▼ An UltraCrinkle textured finish with a standard fired-in coloration help keep the clean lines of this kitchen's design sleek, yet practical. *Interior Design by Brenda Leventhal Interiors. Design and installation by Architectural Annex. Courtesy of UltraGlas®.*

▶ The wave edge on the 3" glass surface references the cabinetry door and drawer fronts throughout this kitchen design. The surface also features a recessed cutting board. *Design by William P. Draper of Draper-DBS™. Glass surface by ThinkGlass.*

▼ Because of the versatility of glass, it can be paired with other countertop surfacing materials. Here, it is paired with glazed Volvic lava stone. *Design by William P. Draper. Glass countertop by ThinkGlass. Lava stone by Pyrolave®.*

◄ Glass can be molded into a diverse range of shapes. Here, a serpent inspires the narrow floating countertop. The floating glass is a great place to serve hors d'oeuvres – use the glass platform as a platter and place them directly on the surface. *Design by William P. Draper. Glass countertop by ThinkGlass.*

▲A glass countertop continues the textural feel of the drawer fronts while serving as a bridge between them and the backsplash. *Design by William P. Draper of Draper-DBS™. Glass countertop by ThinkGlass.*

▶A segmented eating bar gracefully wraps around the windows with a view. The ½" tempered glass has a "shore" texture with elephant glass embellishments. The countertop is mounted on oversized custom-made wood corbels. *Courtesy of UroGlass Design, LLC.*

▲ The stair step designed glass countertop was colored to match the cabinetry. The red glass works with the wall color and upper cabinetry to complete a visual frame around the dark surface island inset, perimeter countertops, and back-splash. *Courtesy of UroGlass Design, LLC.*

▼ A ½" glass countertop set atop a tooled and painted substrate provides an artistic pop in an otherwise neutral kitchen. *Courtesy of UroGlass Design, LLC.*

▲ ▶ A ½" annealed glass countertop with a sweep texture adds depth and drama to a painted substrate. *Courtesy of UroGlass Design, LLC.*

▼ The countertop on this 115" long bar is made of a silvered charcoal annealed glass. A thermo-formed ruffled edge profile makes it even more unique. *Courtesy of UroGlass Design, LLC.*

Edge detail and close-up view of an annealed glass countertop and substrate. *Courtesy of UroGlass Design, LLC.*

▲ ▶ A homeowner's design was fused into this glass countertop, which was carried up to the cabinets with matching backlit panel inserts. *Courtesy of UroGlass Design, LLC.*

An UltraSquiggle texture gives this countertop fluid movement. Two layers – an opaque color layer and a textured layer – were fired and fused into a single material leaving the top surface relatively smooth. *Courtesy of UltraGlas®.*

▲ This tempered charcoal bar countertop has been inverted so that the texture is on top, making it tactile as well as visual. *Courtesy of UroGlass Design, LLC.*

▲ A ½" tempered glass surface floats on stainless steel standoff mounts above a granite countertop. The angled glass countertop has a wire texture. *Courtesy of UroGlass Design, LLC.*

▼ ▶ A homeowner's love of golf is reflected in the golf club shaped glass countertop which floats above a stone surfaced countertop. The design maximizes guest accommodation in a limited area. *Courtesy of UroGlass Design, LLC.*

▶ The drama of the glass countertop continues as wall art. *Courtesy of UltraGlas®.*

◄ A black glass countertop provides a perfect foil for unique accessories. *Courtesy of UltraGlas®.*

▲ A raised glass countertop on an island brings the surface to dining height while the rest of the island remains at a height perfect for food preparation. *Courtesy of UroGlass Design, LLC.*

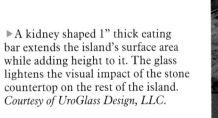

▲Lighting your countertop from beneath will make it the highlight of your kitchen. *Courtesy of ThinkGlass.*

▶A kidney shaped 1" thick eating bar extends the island's surface area while adding height to it. The glass lightens the visual impact of the stone countertop on the rest of the island. *Courtesy of UroGlass Design, LLC.*

▶A working island of granite is surrounded by a sea of ½" thick tempered glass with a rack texture. *Courtesy of UroGlass Design, LLC.*

A vessel sink is framed by a raised glass countertop. *Courtesy of UltraGlas®.*

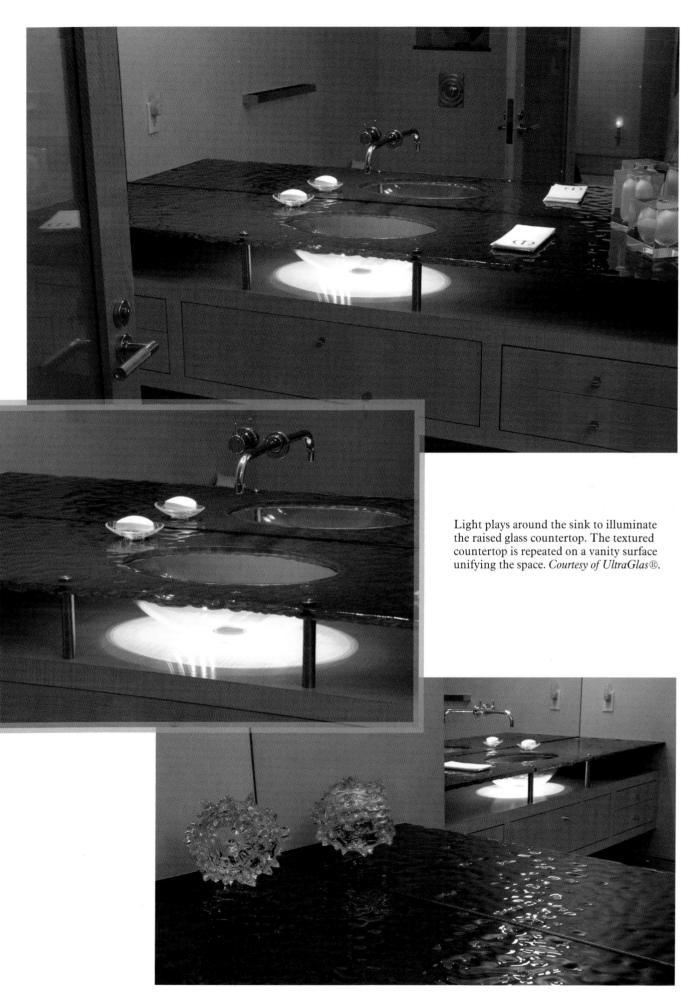

Light plays around the sink to illuminate the raised glass countertop. The textured countertop is repeated on a vanity surface unifying the space. *Courtesy of UltraGlas®.*

▲ The irregular texture of the countertop breaks the sharp, angular lines of the cabinetry. *Courtesy of UltraGlas®.*

▲ Textured glass gives a simple design subtle character. *Courtesy of UroGlass Design, LLC.*

▲ An integrated sink, countertop, and backsplash creates an interesting focal point. *Courtesy of UroGlass Design, LLC.*

▶ The architectural quality of the vanities are center stage with subtle glass countertops – one of which creates a bridge between the two sink areas. *Courtesy of UroGlass Design, LLC.*

▲ This countertop's curvilinear texture is reflected in the vessel sink. *Courtesy of UroGlass Design, LLC.*

▲ A glass topped vanity gives this space an air of glamour reminiscent of the golden age of the silver screen. *Courtesy of UroGlass Design, LLC.*

◀ The veining of this countertop references nature. *Courtesy of UroGlass Design, LLC.*

◄ This glass countertop is reminiscent of softly draped fabric, giving the space a feminine quality. *Courtesy of UroGlass Design, LLC.*

◄ Seashell imprints give the illusion of the sea floor on your countertop. *Courtesy of UroGlass Design, LLC.*

▲ A small countertop can make a huge statement. *Courtesy of Xylem.* ▲

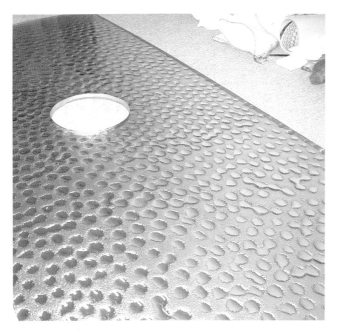

▲ Glass artists can create a texture that reflects your style. *Courtesy of UroGlass Design, LLC.*

▲ A glass countertop with relatively large texture floated above a surface with a smaller pattern adds multiple layers of dimension. *Courtesy of UroGlass Design, LLC.*

▲ A smooth top juxtaposes the rough edge detail of this countertop. *Courtesy of ThinkGlass.*

THE

look of concrete is limited only by your imagination – just about any shape, color, and texture can be achieved. Objects, such as shells, rocks, tree limbs, fiber optic lighting, personal mementos, flecks that sparkle, custom inlays, and trivets can be embedded into the surface. Concrete can develop hairline cracks from natural shrinkage but, for some, this only adds to the charm. The surface can be smooth or textured, shiny or matte. Some surface coloration will get deeper over time.

CONCRETE

About the Material

While most concrete manufacturers have their own proprietary formulas, the basic concrete mix is made of cement, aggregate, sand, water, and air. Some manufacturers use natural and recycled materials in their mix. There are three main techniques used to fabricate a countertop: cast-in-place, pre-cast, and pre-cast glass fiber reinforced concrete (GFRC.)

Cast-in-place countertops are formed and poured on site with a minimum thickness of 1.5". Color can be added with dyes or acid stains. Usually, sinks cannot be integrated when using cast-in-place.

For pre-cast countertops, a template is made of the cabinetry and used to make forms. The 1.5" minimum surface is cast upside down so that when it is taken out of the form and flipped it reveals solid color. To achieve a terrazzo effect, the surface may be ground to expose the aggregate, colored stones, glass or objects that may have been embedded. Any color can be added. Rebar and wire mesh is embedded for strength. Sinks, drain runnels or other special features are easily incorporated.

Pre-cast GFRC is a much stronger and lighter material because it is strengthened with embedded glass fibers. It is formed using the same basic technique as pre-cast concrete. Once removed from the form, it is sprayed with a colored face coat – a slightly altered mix which includes the glass fibers. The glass fibers are also used in the fill-in back coat. The minimum thickness is .75". Any shape, color, embedded objects or special features can be integrated.

What's Good About It

- Heat resistant.
- Unlimited design and color choices.
- Easily customizable to suit your style and preferences.
- Sinks and other special features are easily integrated.

What To Be Aware Of

- Tough on glassware.
- It is porous and needs to be sealed or waxed. However, some manufacturers are developing formulations to alleviate this.
- Some manufacturers recommend trivets to protect the sealant from heat and stains.

Care | Cost

Care
- Use warm, soapy water and a clean soft cloth to clean the surfaces.
- Clean up spills as quickly as possible.
- Avoid abrasives, bleach, and ammonia.
- Some fabricators offer built-in stain resistant options.
- Occasional waxing is necessary to prevent staining.
- For heavier cleaning, use a cleaner made especially for concrete.

Average Cost
- $70 to $200 per square foot, installed.

▲ Multiple components can be fabricated from concrete to create a practical and sophisticated design. Here a concrete bar component in a contrasting color provides drama to the monolithic island. *Courtesy of Flying Turtle Cast Concrete.*

◄ The island's concrete bar component draws the stained wood of the butler's pantry into the main kitchen area, thus unifying the spaces. *Courtesy of the Flying Turtle Cast Concrete.*

▼ More traditional counter shapes – those traditionally used in wood or stone – can easily be formed in concrete. *Courtesy of EarthCrete™ by Sonoma Cast Stone.*

▶ Concrete can be fabricated in various thicknesses to add dimension to a visually light space. Notice the cross corner detail; not only does it add visual interest, it gives just a little extra countertop space for working there. *Courtesy of EarthCrete™ by Sonoma Cast Stone.*

▶ The depth of this concrete countertop varies to accommodate the sink and dishwasher. The thickest area of the apron is an eased 5". It is taupe in color. *Courtesy of Truefrom Concrete, LLC.*

▼ Concrete can be colored, tinted or stained in a wide range of colors and hues. The soft mottled green of this concrete countertop and backsplash easily merges the contemporary reference of the cabinetry with the more rustic feeling of the décor. *Courtesy of Flying Turtle Cast Concrete.*

▲ ▶ A concrete lighted shadowbox draws the eye upwards from the countertop while providing a visual reminder of the material below. The box, like the sink, is framed by embedded seashells. *Courtesy of Flying Turtle Cast Concrete.*

▶ This island's concrete countertop was made as one piece. The forming process allows geometric shapes to be easily incorporated into a design. The color is custom and features light grinding on the rectangular area with heavy grinding on the edges and circular areas. The heavy grinding exposes the recycled glass aggregate for more dimension. *Courtesy of Trueform Concrete, LLC.*

▶ The nature of concrete and its fabrication process makes freeform countertops possible. The countertop shown has a hand-troweled finish; the color is Moss Green. *Courtesy of Trueform Concrete, LLC.*

▶ A mix of hand-troweled and cast concrete form both the countertop and monolithic leg of this workspace. The hand-troweled area is Moss Green; the cast area is Bower Blue. The countertop also features an angled 2" backsplash. *Courtesy of Trueform Concrete, LLC.*

▶ Concrete countertops in the bath are an ideal foil for a vessel sink. *Courtesy of EarthCrete™ by Sonoma Cast Stone.*

◀ An Ash tree branch is inlaid into this hand-troweled concrete countertop. Just about anything you desire can be inlaid into concrete. *Courtesy of Trueform Concrete, LLC.*

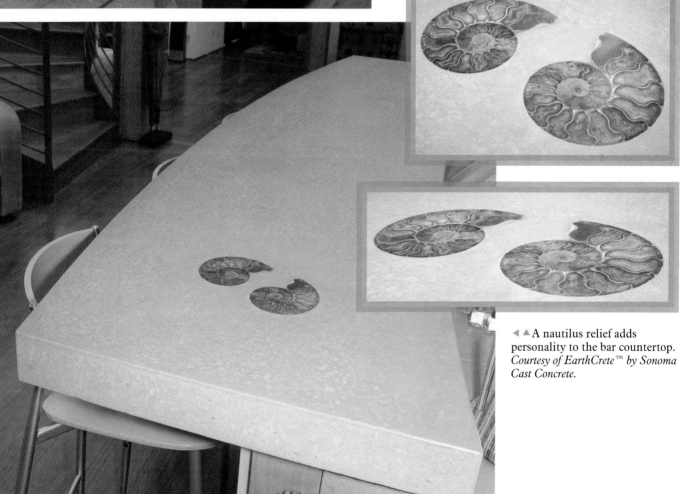

◀ ▲ A nautilus relief adds personality to the bar countertop. *Courtesy of EarthCrete™ by Sonoma Cast Concrete.*

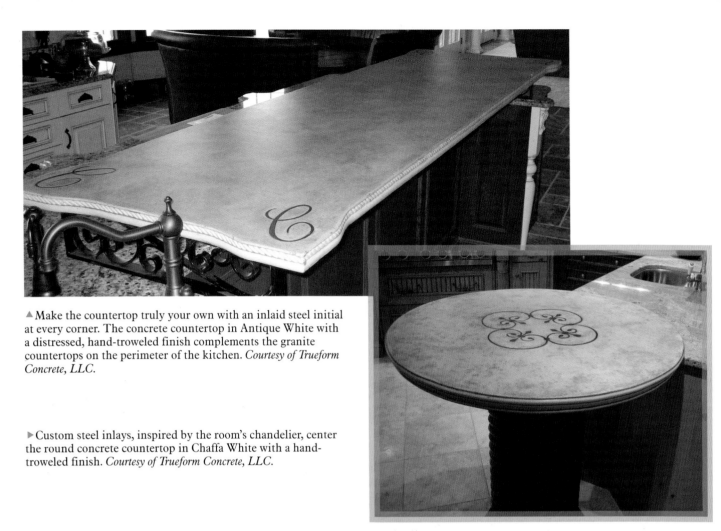

▲ Make the countertop truly your own with an inlaid steel initial at every corner. The concrete countertop in Antique White with a distressed, hand-troweled finish complements the granite countertops on the perimeter of the kitchen. *Courtesy of Trueform Concrete, LLC.*

▶ Custom steel inlays, inspired by the room's chandelier, center the round concrete countertop in Chaffa White with a hand-troweled finish. *Courtesy of Trueform Concrete, LLC.*

▶ This concrete countertop features iron scroll inlays. It is khaki in color with a hand-troweled and distressed finish. The edge profile is a 1.5" classic edge. *Courtesy of Trueform Concrete, LLC.*

▲A farm sink takes a modern twist when integrated into a concrete countertop. The countertop features a chip-faced edge. *Courtesy of Trueform Concrete, LLC.*

▲Integrated sinks in the bath can elevate the utilitarian to the extraordinary. This slant basin sink is large enough for two. *Courtesy of EarthCrete™ by Sonoma Cast Stone.*

◀

Concrete can be a great impersonator. Here, the concrete slabs feature grout lines reminiscent of stone. The countertop also features an integrated farm sink and drainage slant with raised runnels. *Courtesy of EarthCrete™ by Sonoma Cast Stone.*

◀

Countertop conveniences, such as a handy towel bar, make food preparation and clean-up more enjoyable. *Courtesy of Trueform Concrete, LLC.*

Cast in place concrete with integral color.
Courtesy of Keeler Concrete Studio, Inc.

◀Inlaid glass, porcelain, and stones define the integrated sink. *Courtesy of Flying Turtle Cast Concrete.*

◀Your custom sink design can be integrated into a concrete countertop. The curved sink divider gives this sink artsy flair. In addition to the integrated drain slant, the sink is fitted with a sliding mesh panel. The mesh panel can be used as a strainer or can add counter space. *Courtesy of EarthCrete™ by Sonoma Cast Stone.*

◀▼This precast concrete countertop includes an integrated trough sink and integral color. *Courtesy of Keeler Concrete Studio, Inc.*

▼ ▶Special features, such as a his and her trough sink and flush-fronted drawers, can be integrated into a concrete countertop. *Courtesy of Trueform Concrete, LLC.*

▶His and her sinks are easily integrated into a cast concrete countertop. *Courtesy of Flying Turtle Cast Concrete.*

Concrete adds another layer of depth to this monochromatic
design. *Courtesy of Flying Turtle Cast Concrete.*

REPURPOSED
material countertops are as distinctive as the materials from which they are made. They may have a unique look all their own or mimic the look of other material, such as solid soapstone or mosaic. In some cases, you may be able to tell what material – like money – has been repurposed. In other cases, the repurposed material has been completely transformed and is unidentifiable.

repurposed MATERIALS

About the Material

Pre-consumer toilets, glass, money, buttons, cardboard, and newspaper are just a few of the materials that are being repurposed into countertops. For the most part, these materials are combined with a binder of concrete or resin to create the surface. They are as durable as most any other countertop material available. Customization such as adding special features and unique shapes is possible. Some of the materials fabricated from paper are Forest Stewardship Council (FSC) certified.

What's Good About It

- Some meet LEED® requirements.
- Made from recycled post- and pre-consumer materials.
- Very unique – attractive and good for conversation.
- Durable.

What To Be Aware Of

- Some surfaces may be susceptible to scratching.
- Some surfaces may not tolerate high heat.
- Each product has its own needs and properties, consult the manufacturer.

Care | Cost

Care
- For most of the repurposed material countertops, warm soapy water and a soft, clean cloth are all that are required to keep them clean. However, consult the manufacturer for any special instructions.

Average Cost
- $50 and up per square foot, installed.

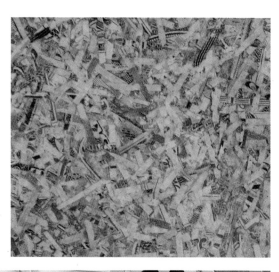

◄ ►
Shredded money is deposited into a countertop. *Courtesy of ShetkaStone.*

▲Another use for old newspapers: recycled into a countertop. *Courtesy of ShetkaStone.*

▲This countertop uses 100% post-consumer curbside recycled glass as a surfacing material with a surprise in every square inch *Courtesy of Vetrazzo. Photo by ©2008 Joel Puliatti for Vetrazzo.*

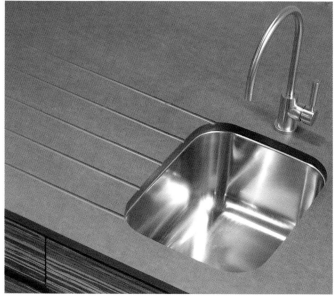

▲This countertop is made from a paper composite material that can be routed with woodworking tools to create a variety of attractive edges and details such as drain boards. *Courtesy of Richlite.*

▲The r50 is made with 50% recycled corrugated cardboard. The material is dense and durable with a natural appeal. *Courtesy of Richlite.*

▲▲The Millifiori or Thousand Flowers is a blend of glassblowers' scraps incorporated into a countertop material. *Courtesy of Vetrazzo. Photo by ©2008 Joel Puliatti for Vetrazzo.*

▲The color produced from recycled cardboard adds warmth to this countertop. *Courtesy of ShetkaStone.*

► ►►The random shapes and colors of this surfacing material recalls Gaudi's trencadis work. (Trencadis refers to a style of mosaic art created from broken and cast-off tile, broken dishes and found objects. The term is from the Catalan language.) *Courtesy of Vetrazzo. Photo by ©2008 Joel Puliatti for Vetrazzo.*

▼This countertop in an office park bathroom in Plano, Texas, is comprised of mixed recycled glass aggregate, recycled reflective glass chips, and crushed porcelain made from pre-consumer, recycled Kohler® toilets and sinks. *Courtesy of EnviroMODE™ by EnviroGLAS®.*

▲This charismatic mix of beverage bottles, with its full spectrum of browns, make this countertop a perfect match for natural wood cabinets; however, it would pop it's top on white enameled cabinetry. *Courtesy of Vetrazzo. Photo by ©2008 Joel Puliatti for Vetrazzo.*

◀Did you trade a few stories with friends last night over a beer or glass of Chardonnay? If so, your empties may end up in a countertop made of recycled glass bottles. *Courtesy of Vetrazzo. Photo by ©2008 Joel Puliatti for Vetrazzo.*

▶ The Richlite Black Diamond paper composite countertops are Forest Stewardship Council (FSC) certified. The material has been a popular surface in the commercial food industry for more than forty years. *Photo by Surface Art Countertops. Courtesy of Richlite.*

▶ Paper composite surfaces were originally used by the aerospace and marine industries as an industrial material more than fifty years ago. Today architects and kitchen designers appreciate the material for its durability and natural appeal. *Courtesy of Richlite.*

▲ Dense and durable paper composite surfaces have been used for a variety of design applications from theater stages to skate park ramps. Kitchen countertops are one of the most popular uses due to the material's attractive matte finish and sustainable appeal. *Courtesy of Richlite.*

▲ Because of the density of paper composites, kitchen designers can create long spans and dramatic cantilevers without adding extra support. Paper composite countertops come in a variety of thicknesses to suit any design. *Courtesy of Richlite.*

▲ Paper composites have been a popular cutting board material for more than forty years. The paper composite material can be shaped with standard woodworking tools to create beautiful and functional kitchen accents such as chopping blocks. *Photo by Starrow Enterprises. Courtesy of Richlite.*

◀ *Innovative Home Magazine's* Green Home in Forth Worth, Texas, featured a countertop made of mixed recycled glass aggregate and crushed porcelain made from pre-consumer, recycled Kohler® toilets and sinks. *Courtesy of EnviroMODE™ by EnviroGLAS®.*

◀ Whole Foods Spa chose this countertop for their Spa in Dallas, Texas. It features mixed recycled glass aggregate and crushed porcelain made from pre-consumer, recycled Kohler® toilets and sinks. *Courtesy of EnviroMODE™ by EnviroGLAS®.*

◄ ▲ This countertop was installed in the Noyola family's Chicago home for ABC's Extreme Makeover/Home Edition. The countertop contains mixed recycled glass aggregate along with crushed porcelain made from pre-consumer, recycled Kohler® toilets and sinks. *Courtesy of EnviroMODE™ by EnviroGLAS®.*

◄ Recycled glass aggregate, along with recycled mother-of-pearl buttons, comprise this residential countertop. *Courtesy of EnviroSLAB™ by EnviroGLAS®.*

◄ The active pattern in the countertop provides a subtle contrast to the sleek contemporary faucet and sink. *Courtesy of Vetrazzo. Photo by ©2008 Joel Puliatti for Vetrazzo.*

▼ The countertop in this Chicago residence is made from custom colored resin along with crushed porcelain made from pre-consumer, recycled Kohler® toilets and sinks. *Courtesy of EnviroMODE™ by EnviroGLAS®.*

This countertop installation is at the PepsiCo office building in Rogers, Arkansas. The countertop contains recycled glass aggregate along with recycled mother-of-pearl buttons. *Courtesy of EnviroSLAB™ by EnviroGLAS®.*

The recycled blue glass compliments the solid field tiles of the backsplash – an effective way to add pattern. *Courtesy of Vetrazzo. Photo by ©2008 Joel Puliatti for Vetrazzo.*

ENGINEERED

stone gives you the look and feel of natural stone such as granite, marble, travertine, and concrete, but with more color choices. However, it lacks the unique veining, color, and pattern variations of natural stone – the coloring and patterns are extremely uniform. A wide variety of colors in shiny and matte finishes are available.

About the Material

This extremely durable material is made by combining natural crushed stone with pigments and resin. Typically, the mixture is 93 percent quartz (one of nature's hardest minerals) and 7 percent pigment and resin. The resin makes it more durable and easier to care for than natural stone. Though most engineered stone surfaces do not require sealing, some made with marble or other soft stone aggregates may require a sealant. The material is installed in slabs that need to be pre-fabricated and pre-cut.

What's Good About It

- Non-porous; hygienic and virtually stain-proof.
- Extremely durable: scratch and chip resistant.
- Heat resistant.
- Easy to maintain.
- Pattern is consistent throughout, making it easy to match seams.

What To Be Aware Of

- Less natural looking than slab stone.
- If composed of marble and some other softer stones, it may need sealing.
- It can crack with extremely rapid temperature changes.
- Though it's ideal for large areas, it may look manufactured due to its lack of inconsistencies.
- Cutting on the surface may dull knives; cutting boards are recommended.

Care | Cost

Care
- Clean with a damp cloth or paper towel and nonabrasive liquid detergent.
- Most engineered stone surfaces don't require sealing or waxing.

Average Cost
- $75 and up per square foot, installed

◀The skewed planes of this island's countertops break up the straight lines of the cabinetry, hardware, and perimeter countertops. *Courtesy of Cambria.*

◀▲This countertop continues the warmth of the stained wood cabinetry of this serving surface. The curvilinear trough sink makes the countertop multi-purposeful… it can be used as a sink or filled with ice to serve bottled beverages. *Courtesy of Cambria.*

▲▼The deep gray of this surface is inspired by concrete. The different thicknesses of the countertops in these two images illustrate how different the same surface can appear. *Courtesy of CaesarStone.*

▲A close-up of engineered stone inspired by concrete. *Courtesy of CaesarStone.*

▲The gray island countertop helps soften the lines between the gray décor elements of the living space and the kitchen's perimeter countertops of black. *Courtesy of Cambria.*

▲The warm red Ruby Reflections color of this countertop is continued on an accent wall to make an eye-popping statement. This particular color contains recycled content. *Courtesy of CaesarStone.*

▶The unexpected combination of gray countertops and stained cabinetry create a most sophisticated urban appearance. *Courtesy of Cambria.*

◄A crisp Fresh White countertop provides a European feel to this kitchen's clean design aesthetic. *Courtesy of CaesarStone.*

▲▼The white on white aesthetic of the perimeter cabinetry and countertops provides a wonderful foil to show your personality through accessories, art or even a unique island topped with a contrasting countertop. The white countertop paired with a white sink and cabinetry keeps the design fresh and airy. *Courtesy of CaesarStone.*

▼Special edge details on the countertops surrounding a simple farm sink can elevate its importance. *Courtesy of CaesarStone.*

◀ The juxtaposition of dark and light add drama to the space while paying complement to the brick walls. *Courtesy of Cambria.*

◀ If you like the feel of an all white kitchen – cabinetry, appliances, and countertops – but think it may be too stark for you, consider using a gray countertop and stainless appliances to soften the starkness. *Courtesy of CaesarStone.*

◀ Mixing countertop surfaces is a great way of defining space. Here a butcher's block topped island is identified as a preparation station, while the stone-topped island is more elaborate, perfect for serving. Notice too that the color of the front-most island's countertop refers back to the stone hood, increasing the importance of the piece to the room's overall design. *Courtesy of Cambria.*

◀ A large island with lots of work surface is perfect for an open loft space. *Courtesy of Cambria.*

◀ Using the same countertop surface on differently finished cabinetry can unite the space, especially if it is a large area. *Courtesy of Cambria.*

◀ The mottled, granite-like appearance of the island surface grounds the red décor accents – backsplash, upholstery, rug, and shades. *Courtesy of Cambria.*

▲ A classic combination: black and white. It's simple and elegant. *Courtesy of Cambria.*

▼ The soft muted tones of the stone hearth, island, and walls are echoed in the countertop. *Courtesy of Cambria.*

◄ The rich Flint Black countertop plays well against the cherry cabinetry – reminiscent of the Biedermeier style. *Courtesy of Cambria.*

▼ The island's countertop, with flecks of browns and whites, unite the stark contrast of the stained and painted cabinetry. *Courtesy of Cambria.*

▲ ▶ The red countertop punctuates the
green cabinetry to create a unique retro look.
Courtesy of CaesarStone.

◄ ▲ A bright red countertop emphasizes the design importance of the island. The manner in which the countertop joins the island base adds to the theatrical appeal of the piece. *Courtesy of CaesarStone.*

▼ The red countertop reinforces the Mondrian inspiration of this design. *Courtesy of CaesarStone.*

▲Bright blue countertops add personality and
style to a very traditional cabinetry style and space.
Courtesy of Quartz by Staron®.

▲These countertops will make it feel like Spring all year.▲
What a wonderful and energizing greeting when you come home.
Courtesy of CaesarStone.

▲The thick blue heavily patterned countertop unites the textures of the other materials of the space. *Courtesy of CaesarStone.*

▲A vivid green quartz countertop atop white cabinetry blends today's style sensibility with a retro inspired kitchen. *Courtesy of CaesarStone.*

▲Today's retro feeling is made more complete with vivid green countertops. *Courtesy of CaesarStone.*

▼ ▶ The dappled countertop seems to bring in the treetops of the surrounding countryside. A raised section in the middle of the island is topped with the same surfacing as the work surface. The section creates a break between the sink and provides an electrical source or space for a docking station. *Courtesy of Cambria.*

▶ The choice of countertops keep this contemporary design warm and friendly. *Courtesy of Cambria.*

▲A floating glass countertop provides a frosted frame to the countertop below. The island's countertop features the same tones as in the backsplash tile. *Courtesy of Cambria.*

▼A deep blue countertop reinforces this classic, elegant design. *Courtesy of Cambria.*

▶Glazed Volvic lava stone is fired to 1000°C, which creates a delicate crazing in the enamel during the cooling process. Lava stone is extracted from quarries and tends to be a consistent and dense stone. *Courtesy of Pyrolave®.*

◄ ▲ The earthy tones of the countertop keep the design honest to its Arts & Crafts' influence. *Courtesy of Cambria.*

◄ The rich brown mottled surface of Jerusalem Sand envelopes this island to create a monolithic aesthetic. *Courtesy of CaesarStone.*

◄ The simple cabinetry makes the island countertop the center of attention. *Courtesy of Cambria.*

▲ ▶The rough layered edge treatment of the island countertop adds just the right contrast to the tailored design of the kitchen's other elements. *Courtesy of Cambria.*

▼Engineered stone provides a practical serving surface while mimicking the surrounding wall. *Courtesy of Cambria.*

▲The right countertop choice perpetuates the desired aesthetic. *Courtesy of Cambria.*

◀The contrasting light and dark countertops make each area seem like separate spaces within the room. *Courtesy of Cambria.*

▲Detail of the rough cut edge. *Courtesy of CaesarStone.*

▲The neutral countertop allows the rich wood cabinetry to be the star of this room. *Courtesy of Cambria.*

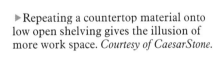
▲White countertops combined with
stained wood cabinetry is ideal for an
open floor plan loft. *Courtesy of Cambria.*

▶Repeating a countertop material onto
low open shelving gives the illusion of
more work space. *Courtesy of CaesarStone.*

◄ The cool, contemporary feeling of the stainless steel appliances and seating continues on the engineered stone countertops. *Courtesy of CaesarStone.*

▲ This countertop continues the tone of the cabinetry to create a continuous vertical line. *Courtesy of Cambria.*

◄ Engineered stone provides a surface durable enough to withstand the demands of a heavily used coffee station. *Courtesy of Cambria.*

▶A deep countertop compliments the heavy wood cabinetry while reflecting the under mount lighting to brighten the space. *Courtesy of Cambria.*

▲A metal edge detail echoes the cabinetry hardware. *Courtesy of CaesarStone.*

▲ Bi-level countertops are ideal for carrying on conversation or helping with homework. *Courtesy of CaesarStone.*

▲ The soft grey countertop reflects the room's fireplace focal point. *Courtesy of Quartz by Staron®.*

▲ A low countertop adds a splash of color as well as providing an area for dining or serving. *Courtesy of CaesarStone.*

▲ Engineered stone provides the aesthetic of natural stone without care and maintenance concerns of some natural stones. *Courtesy of Cambria.*

▲ A white countertop helps to heighten the impact of the bright blue cabinets. *Courtesy of CaesarStone.*

▲ The soft hue of the countertops add to the serenity of the spa-like bath. An intricate edge detail adds to the elegance. *Courtesy of Cambria.*

▶ Tone on tone cabinetry and countertops provide a clean palette for accessories. *Courtesy of CaesarStone.*

◀ A cantilevered countertop with a smooth glossy top and rough cut edge gives a sophisticated urban feel. *Courtesy of Cambria.*

◄ A vessel sink, contemporary faucet, and bright blue countertop add a modern flair to traditional cabinetry. *Courtesy of CaesarStone.*

◄ A detailed countertop edge makes an island appear as a furniture piece ready for serving guests – no table linens needed. *Courtesy of CaesarStone.*

▼ A classic edge detail keeps the countertop and cabinetry in harmony. *Courtesy of CaesarStone.*

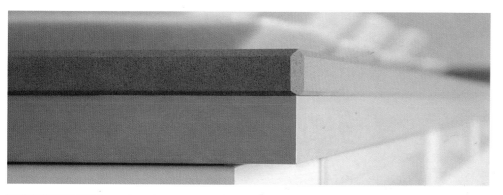

◀ Setting a countertop atop a complimentary material creates an interesting and unique apron. *Courtesy of CaesarStone.*

◀ A double bullnose edge detail on a thick countertop is bold enough to stand up to the heavily carved island. *Courtesy of CaesarStone.*

◀ Detail of a beveled countertop. *Courtesy of CaesarStone.*

▲ Flecks in the countertop catch the light and sparkle, reinforcing the shine of the stainless cooktop and drawer hardware. *Courtesy of CaesarStone.*

▲ A bullnose edge softens this countertop. *Courtesy of CaesarStone.*

▲ Engineered stone incorporates complimentary colored flecks into the field tones. *Courtesy of CaesarStone.*

▲Engineered stone cut into tiles and set on the bias with grout lines. *Courtesy of CaesarStone.*

▲Engineered stone is available in varying thicknesses to enhance a design. *Courtesy of CaesarStone.*

▲A metal band inlay. *Courtesy of CaesarStone.*

◀An example of a classic beveled edge. *Courtesy of Cambria.*

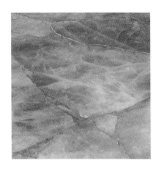

Ultimate

luxury and opulence best describes extreme engineered stone surfacing fabricated with semi-precious gemstones and fossils. The fire and brilliance of the semi-precious gemstones is extraordinary – offering the look of intricate jewelry or the finest fabric. Some of the stones are translucent and can be backlit to display beautiful veining and coloring.

Extreme

engineered **STONE**

About the Material

Extreme engineered stone surfaces are made of natural, semi-precious stones and fossils, which are individually cut using some of the same techniques as jewelers and bound to form a continuous countertop. The rough stones are hand-cut, matched, and set. The type of cuts used, typically a thin slice, enhance the vibrant hues and brilliance of the stones.

What's Good About It

- Heat, stain and scratch resistant.
- Extremely unique aesthetic.
- Can tolerate moderately hot temperatures though trivets are recommended.

What To Be Aware Of

- Expensive.
- Avoid using sharp objects directly on the countertop.
- Use an insulated hot pad when using cooking units, e.g. electric skillets, placed directly on the countertop.

Care | Cost

Care
- Wipe using warm water, mild detergent and a white cloth.
- Avoid caustic cleaning agents.

Average Cost
- $200 and up, per square foot, installed.

▶ The breathtaking pattern of banded and contoured browns give this crystal its distinctive quality. Brown Agate has traditionally been sought after for its protective powers. *Courtesy of Concetto® by CaesarStone.*

◄ Lighting a countertop from underneath adds depth and visual appeal. It will also change the appearance of the material dramatically while providing a source of ambient light. *Courtesy of Majestic Gemstone.*

◄ ▲ Profound desert landscapes call to us from the natural shades of the Jasper crystal. The warm earth tones of this stone inspire creative contemplation and innovative thinking. *Courtesy of Concetto® by CaesarStone.*

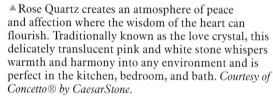

▲Rose Quartz creates an atmosphere of peace and affection where the wisdom of the heart can flourish. Traditionally known as the love crystal, this delicately translucent pink and white stone whispers warmth and harmony into any environment and is perfect in the kitchen, bedroom, and bath. *Courtesy of Concetto® by CaesarStone.*

◄A backlit amethyst countertop punches up the everyday routine as well as adding purple drama to a celebration. Amethyst is said to increase courage, intuition, and creativity while balancing the energy centers of our body and providing a soothing and calming influence. *Courtesy of Majestic Gemstone.*

◄Tiger's Eye is perfect for a family-centered island countertop. It brings protection and good luck; soothes nervousness; and helps concentration (perfect for homework time). *Courtesy of Majestic Gemstone.*

▲Gray Agate adds elegance to a design – whether traditional or modern. Its unique circular patterning of warm and cool tones gives this translucent gray and white crystal its gently sophisticated look. According to tradition, agates generate positive energy and promote progress. *Courtesy of Concetto® by CaesarStone.*

▲The delicate, barely visible white patterns in this crystal capture the essence of sunlight on northern glaciers. White Quartz radiates purity and serenity. It is the ultimate look in modern design as it can be complemented by either dark or light accessories. *Courtesy of Concetto® by CaesarStone.*

▶The gemstone countertop completes the furniture look of this bathroom vanity. *Courtesy of Majestic Gemstone.*

◄ A white quartz peninsula – countertop and support – accentuates the linearity of this kitchen. White Quartz is said to purify, energize, contribute to developing awareness, motivate action, heal emotionally, and is important for self-esteem. *Courtesy of Majestic Gemstone.*

▲ This island features a semi-precious gemstone countertop of white quartz. *Courtesy of Concetto® by CaesarStone.*

◄ The raised white quartz countertop seems to float above the black lower counter. *Courtesy of Concetto® by CaesarStone.*

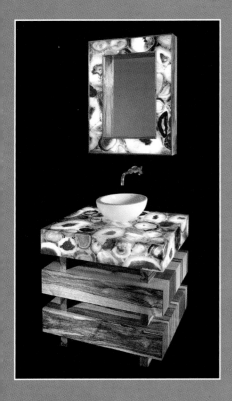

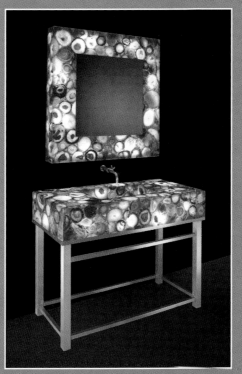

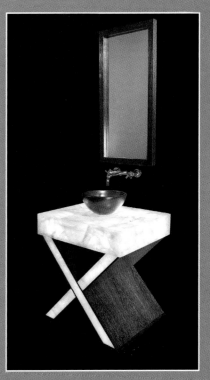

A lighted countertop and matching details such as a mirror surround, shelves, and stand, show the beauty of the stone from which the material is made. It also provides ambient lighting. *Courtesy of Majestic Gemstone.*

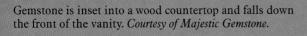

Gemstone is inset into a wood countertop and falls down the front of the vanity. *Courtesy of Majestic Gemstone.*

WOOD

gives a warm look and homey feeling. It is as at home in a contemporary setting as it is in a traditional design. The material will dent and scratch, but some think that only adds character. Wood can balance the coolness of stainless steel appliances while complimenting other materials such as laminates and natural or engineered stone. Simple and intricate patterns are available and can be customized. Species can be mixed to create your own look. Reclaimed woods from riverbeds or razed buildings are available.

About the Material

Wood countertops are made of wood segments glued together and planed until smooth. How the wood is arranged and the grain is situated determines the aesthetic and strength of the material. There are three grain types: face grain, where the width of the wood plank is visible; edge grain, where the wood planks are placed on edge; and end grain, where the wood is cut into blocks and arranged so that the cut end points up. Wood countertops can vary in thickness from 1.25" to 6".

Many species, with myriad color, grains, and prices are available. Some of the most common species include oak, cherry, walnut, maple, teak, wenge, bamboo, African mahogany, and zebrawood.

What's Good About It

- Won't hurt knives; can cut on the surface.
- Damaged areas can be sanded and refinished.
- Wood adds warmth to a room.
- Hygienic with proper care; easy to clean.
- Glassware friendly.
- Long service for a relatively low cost.
- Many manufacturers follow Forest Stewardship Council (FSC) guidelines.

What To Be Aware Of

- Moisture: wood expands when wet and shrinks as it dries, causing unsightly and unhygienic cracks and fissures.
- Prone to burn marks and staining.
- Needs to be oiled or sealed.
- Standing water can darken wood.
- Scratches must be oiled or sealed.

Care | Cost

Care
- Wash with warm soapy water and a clean cloth immediately after use.
- Bleach and abrasives may harm the surface.
- Avoid letting the wood crack, as that's were bacteria collects.
- High use areas can be sanded and refinished.
- Periodic sealing or oiling to avoid water damage is required.

Average Cost
- $50 to $200 per square foot, installed.

▲The feeling of the perimeter stone countertops and the knee-wall's countertop seem to merge into the island's butcher block surface. The 16' long maple and wenge checkerboard countertop becomes the design focal point for this space. *Photography by Tom Gutekunst. Courtesy of The Grothouse Lumber Company.*

◄Part of the fun of butcher block countertops is mixing and matching wood. Shown here is a random species mix of end grains. *Courtesy of The Grothouse Lumber Company.*

▲ ▶ Reclaimed wood offers an inherent character difficult to recreate in new wood. Shown here is Jarrah wood reclaimed from old warehouses in the Perth area of Australia. *Courtesy of Trestlewood*®.

◄ The planks and graining of the cherry wood used in this countertop add dimension to the simple white cabinetry. *Courtesy of The Grothouse Lumber Company, installed by The Countertop Factory.*

▼ A solid cherry countertop keeps the design clean yet elegant. *Courtesy of The Grothouse Lumber Company, installed by The Countertop Factory.*

◄ A single species wooden countertop combined with a complex edge profile, such as the Roman Edge shown here, adds quiet elegance to a space. *Courtesy of The Grothouse Lumber Company.*

▲ A checkerboard countertop on the island adds a playful touch to the traditional blue and white tile above the cooking station. Design by Mary S. Mitchell of MES Mitchell Interiors, LLC. *Courtesy of The Grothouse Lumber Company.*

▶ The island's countertop relates to the flooring which picks up the tones of the range hood to create a harmonious space. *Design by Jessica Hetrich, ASID of Kountry Kraft, Inc. Courtesy of The Grothouse Lumber Company.*

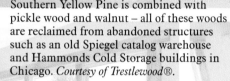

Southern Yellow Pine is combined with pickle wood and walnut – all of these woods are reclaimed from abandoned structures such as an old Spiegel catalog warehouse and Hammonds Cold Storage buildings in Chicago. *Courtesy of Trestlewood®.*

◄Every piece of reclaimed rough hewn wood is unique. Here, it is used as a powder room countertop. *Courtesy of Trestlewood®.*

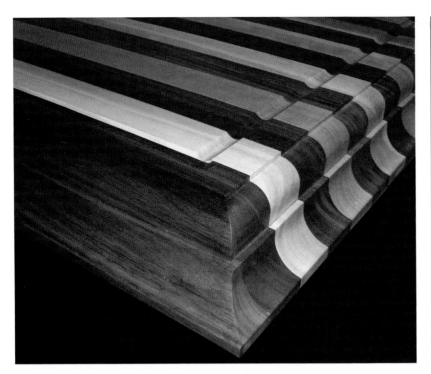

▲ Walnut, maple, and cherry is used together in a striped design. A juice runnel carved around the perimeter of the countertop catches any liquids. The intricate edge profile emphasizes the grandeur of the design. *Courtesy of The Grothouse Lumber Company.*

▲ Cherry, wenge, and Brazilian Cherry create a very sop[?] frame design. *Courtesy of The Grothouse Lumber Company.*

▲ The classic Greek Key design is combined with a traditional checkerboard. *Courtesy of The Grothouse Lumber Company.*

▲ The beauty of walnut enhances this simple butcher block design. *Courtesy of The Grothouse Lumber Company.*

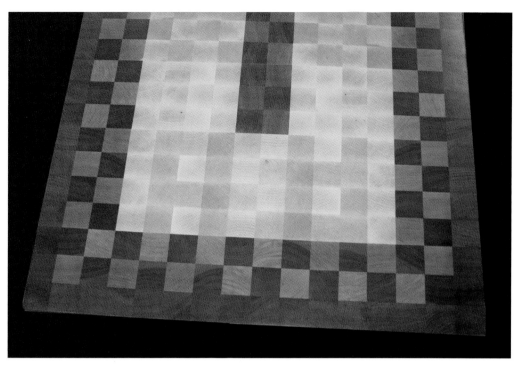

▲ This unique checkerboard design features a multi-species combination. An African Mahogany center is surrounded by maple, which is framed by two rows of cherry and walnut checkerboard, and edged with a row of teak. *Courtesy of The Grothouse Lumber Company.*

▲ A close-up of the maple and wenge checkerboard design. *Courtesy of The Grothouse Lumber Company.*

▲Wood countertops can be made to just about any shape or size you desire. *Cabinetry and design by Auer Kitchens. Courtesy of The Grothouse Lumber Company.*

◄ ▼Circle and square, light and dark combine for a sophisticatedly serene space. *Design by Jennifer Gilmer Kitchen & Bath. Courtesy of The Grothouse Lumber Company.*

◀ ▲Tones from the lower stone
countertop blend with the wood bar
countertop and unite the surrounding
wall cabinetry. *Design by Mary Hines
of Shenendoah Millwork. Courtesy of
The Grothouse Lumber Company.*

BOTH

soapstone and slate can provide a very sleek look when they are polished or oiled, or a more rustic feel when left unpolished or treated. While slight variation in color is uncommon, a rich and interesting patina can develop when these surfaces are not treated.

SOAPSTONE & SLATE

About the Materials

Soapstone is composed mainly of mineral talc and often has striations of quartz. The color is generally dark grey with limited variations; however, oiling will give soapstone a deep, rich glow and if left natural, it will develop a unique patina. It is available in .75" to 2.75" slabs.

Slate is formed from clay on ancient seabeds. The most common colors are grey, black, rust, green, and purple.

What's Good About It

- Relatively low maintenance.
- Family friendly.
- Low to non-porous; hygienic.
- Heat resistant and durable with care.
- Oiling is optional.
- Sinks can be integrated.

What To Be Aware Of

- Limited colors.
- Very soft; susceptible to scratching.
- Scratches and chips easily especially on edges, but they can be sanded out.
- Hard on glassware.

Care | Cost

Care
- Clean with mild soap and water.
- Periodic oiling will make the surface shine; but oiling is optional.

Average Cost
- $70 to $200 per square foot, installed.

▲The character of natural, non-oiled soapstone continuously changes with use. *Courtesy of ©Green Mountain Soapstone Corp.*

◀The soapstone used in this kitchen features grey tones with dramatic light and dark crystals. The homeowners like the look and feel of the soapstone so much that they used it on the countertops and floors as well as the material for a farmhouse sink. *Courtesy of ©Green Mountain Soapstone Corp.*

▶The farmhouse sink is made of the same material as the countertops, natural, non-oiled soapstone. *Courtesy of ©Green Mountain Soapstone Corp.*

▲This modern kitchen design mixes both oiled and non-oiled soapstone. Non-oiled soapstone used as the backsplash counterbalances with oiled soapstone used on the countertops; note the carved runnels by the sink for drainage. *Courtesy of ©Green Mountain Soapstone Corp.*

▲Significant veining in some soapstone's surface can reinforce the style of a kitchen. Here, the veining adds to the rustic feel of the space. *Courtesy of ©Green Mountain Soapstone Corp.*

◀Hand carved corbels support the soapstone countertop. Incorporating details made of the same materials creates continuity. *Courtesy of ©Green Mountain Soapstone Corp.*

▶Jade green slate is used here to create a unified feeling between the family area and the kitchen. The integrated slate sink continues the look without adding another material component. *Woodland Jade Slate™ from Vermont courtesy of ©RMG Stone Products, Inc.*

▶Heavily carved cabinetry is enhanced with the richness of soapstone. *Courtesy of ©Green Mountain Soapstone Corp.*

▲Slate countertops were used in a 1950s kitchen renovation. The rounded corners of the peninsula are reminiscent of the era, but the material updates the feeling. *Woodland Jade Slate™ from Vermont courtesy of ©RMG Stone Products, Inc.*

▲The rounded corners of the sink surround refers to the retro rounded peninsula. Details such as these help to bring together design elements. *Courtesy of ©Green Mountain Soapstone Corp.*

◀▲The purple hues in the slate countertop reinforce the Arts & Crafts style of the room. *Mountain Plum Slate™ courtesy of ©RMG Stone Products, Inc.*

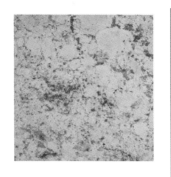

VERSATILE

granite and marble meld with any design - contemporary or traditional - with timeless, natural style. Typically, both have active patterning, color variation, and veining or markings that give them their distinctive character. There are thousands of colors available. No two slabs are alike, so it may be difficult to match. This variation makes it fun to choose your own slabs. Finishes include polished, honed, and matte.

GRANITE & MARBLE

About the Materials

Both granite and marble are natural stones mined throughout the world. Granite's shimmer comes from quartz crystals, mica, and feldspar trapped when the stone was formed by volcanic activity. Marble is formed from limestone that is exposed to heat and pressure in the earth's crust. The characteristic veining and color of marble varies by location and type of impurities trapped during its formation.

What's Good About It

What's Good About It

Granite
- No two countertops look the same.
- Extremely durable; most knives won't scratch it.
- Heat resistant; but use hot pads as a precaution.
- Wide range of colors and patterns.
- Chips and scratches can be repaired.
- Timeless style.
- One of the hardest surfaces available.

Marble
- Every countertop is unique.
- Durable
- Timeless style.
- Good for bakers; provides a cool surface for handling dough.
- Long lasting if cared for properly.

What To Be Aware Of

Granite
- Tough on dishware and glasses.
- Difficult to match sections.
- Requires a penetrating sealer; every 6-months recommended.
- Acidic and oily substances may stain.

Marble
- Excessive or repeated exposure to heat can leave scars.
- Soft and porous.
- Needs regular waxing and sealing.
- Excessive and repeated exposure to heat can leave scars or burn marks.
- Acidic substances may etch the surface.

Care | Cost

Care

Granite
- Everyday clean up with damp cloth and non-abrasive, mild liquid detergent or cleaner specially formulated for granite.
- Blot spills immediately.
- Avoid bleach and other caustic cleaners such as vinegar, ammonia, degreasers, and citrus cleaners.

Care

Marble
- Easy everyday clean up with a clean cloth or soft sponge and warm water.
- Buff until it shines.
- Avoid bleach and other caustic cleaners such as vinegar, ammonia, degreasers, and citrus cleaners.

Average Cost
- $50 to $200 per square foot, installed.

▲

The random dark veining of the granite breaks the linearity of the cabinetry, hardware, plank flooring, and floor plan of this kitchen. *Brazilian Alpana Cream granite courtesy of GerrityStone™. Photography by John Horner Photography.*

▶ The neutrality of white marble mixes well with other countertop materials. Bianco Carrara marble helps to draw the eye to the room's focal point, a custom butcher block. *Courtesy of Everlife™ by Innovative Stone.*

▶ White cabinetry topped with Bianco Carrara marble creates an ideal canvas that allows colorful accents to pop. *Courtesy of Everlife™ by Innovative Stone.*

◄ Granite mixes well with other surface materials. A backsplash of complementary colored ceramic tile set on a bias reflects in the polished surface of the countertop and adds additional depth to the granite. *Labrador Blue granite courtesy of Everlife™ by Innovative Stone.*

◄ A marble topped island is ideal for those who enjoy candy and pastry making. The inherent coolness of the stone helps regulate the temperature of your delicious creation. *Bianco Carrara marble courtesy of Everlife™ by Innovative Stone.*

▼ Drain slots can be custom cut into a marble countertop to make clean up easier. *Bianco Carrara marble courtesy of Everlife™ by Innovative Stone.*

▼ ▶ Marble can be used to create any mood you desire – traditional to modern. *Bianco Carrara marble courtesy of Everlife™ by Innovative Stone.*

◀ Two slabs of stone are *booked* to create an interesting corner treatment. Booking can also be used on long spans. *Courtesy of GerrityStone™*.

◀▲ A traditional blue and white kitchen color scheme becomes very dynamic when the blue is provided by granite countertops. *Labrador Blue granite courtesy of Everlife™ by Innovative Stone.*

◀▲No two granite countertops are alike – even if the slabs are quarried from the same area. Natural deposits of minerals and crystals, along with the earth's pressure, create unique markings. Intricate edge profiles draw attention to the unique patterns throughout each slab of granite. *Labrador Blue courtesy of Everlife™ by Innovative Stone.*

◀Green granite adds a bit of the exotic to an otherwise traditional kitchen. Shown is Tropic Green granite from India with veining reminiscent of the Aurora Borealis. *Courtesy of Everlife™ by Innovative Stone.*

▲The variation of pattern and color in granite can help unite different cabinetry colors to accomplish a desired style. The Verde Butterfly granite is quarried from Brazil. The deep green stone boasts white crystallization accented with fine gold veining and occasional garnet flecks. *Courtesy of Everlife™ by Innovative Stone.*

◀The earthy browns and golden green undertones in Tropic Brown granite from Saudi Arabia work well with a large selection of woods, especially those with a golden tone. Consider using it with sage green or yellow painted cabinetry. *Courtesy of Everlife™ by Innovative Stone.*

▲Giallo Veneziano from Brazil works well with almost any décor. The crystalline deposits mixed with rich earthy tones add an occasional sparkle when the light hits it. Used with Tuscan sunset orange walls and cherry cabinetry it creates a warm and friendly atmosphere. *Courtesy of Everlive™ by Innovative Stone.*

▲Ubatuba is a rich, deep black-green granite with natural gold crystallization from Espirito Santo. It works especially well with natural wood floors and cabinetry. *Courtesy of Everlife™ by Innovative Stone.*

◀Absolute Black is just that – absolutely black. It is beautiful either polished or honed. This granite works in either a traditional or contemporary style. It is also a great complement to more active granites, such as Giallo Veneziano; consider using one on the perimeter countertops and the other on an island. *Courtesy of Everlife™ by Innovative Stone.*

◀Rich veining flows through the Yellow Bamboo granite, creating a sense of movement in the room. *Design by William P. Draper. Courtesy of Draper-DBS™.*

◀ ▶ The sea foam green granite adds to the springtime fresh aesthetic of this kitchen. The granite has shades of lilac, blue, and peach, which work well with the powder blue of the ceiling, winter white cabinetry, and high gloss wood floor. *Indian granite courtesy of GerrityStone™. Photo by Eric Roth Photography.*

◀ ▲ Mineral and crystal deposits give granite its distinct look. For example, white and ivory toned granites can be dramatically different depending on what part of the world they are quarried. *Bianco and Golden Ivory marbles courtesy of Everlife™ by Innovative Stone.*

▲ The traditional black granite has been torched, beaten, and then brushed to create the look of antique leather. A smooth, decorative edge makes the textured surface really pop, giving the appearance of old and new. The smooth edges match and compliment the solid stone sinks. *Courtesy of GerrityStone™. Photography by Shelly Harrison Photography.*

▲ This project features two different stones: Juparana Bourdeaux Super with ruby reds, auburns, copper, and tangerine tones and a cheery Spring Green granite on the island. *Courtesy of GerrityStone™. Photo by Shelly Harrison Photography.*

DEPENDING on the type

of metal chosen for a countertop, it can be a workhorse or a show horse so to speak. Stainless steel for example is extremely durable and can stand up to heavy work while copper is softer and perhaps isn't the first choice for a high use area. However, both can stand up to high design expectations with various finishes, texturing, and patinas. Keep in mind that metal countertops aren't solid. Typically, sheets of the metal are fastened to a wood or similar backing material. The edges are wrapped around the backing material and the corners welded and ground to the point where they are unnoticeable. Metals pair easily with wood and warmer stone surfaces.

About the Materials

Stainless steel is an alloy of steel, nickel, and chromium. Sheets of the material are available in various gauges or thicknesses; use a 16-gauge or thicker to prevent warping. It is graded according to its resistance to corrosion, staining, maintenance, cost, and luster; number 304 is the best kitchen grade. Stainless steel finishes are also classified by number, indicating the amount of polish and reflectivity; the higher the number, the higher the polish and reflectivity. Highly polished surfaces will show scuffs and fingerprints as well as reflect a lot of light. To prevent dents, it should be mounted on plywood.

Copper is one of the softest metals used for countertops. It will turn a rich golden brown with age or any number of patinas can be achieved. Its properties are naturally anti-bacterial.

Zinc is a soft metal that has been used for wash basins, cooking surfaces, and countertops since the early twentieth century. Though it starts shiny, it will develop a blue-grey pewter-like finish with slight hints of a green patina.

Pewter is an alloy of mostly tin (85-95 percent) and a small amount of copper and other metals such as bismuth or antimony. It is the softest of the countertop materials. Though some pewter contains lead, food grade pewter used as countertops does not. Its silvery color ages to a duller grey.

What's Good About It

Stainless Steel
- Very low maintenance; easy clean up.
- Non-porous; inhospitable to bacteria.
- Resistant to heat, moisture, stains, and rust.
- Resistant to dents; the heavier the gauge, the more resistant.
- Slight scratches can be polished to a soft patina.
- Impervious to acids and oils.
- Sinks can be integrated.
- Can be recycled.

Copper
- Naturally anti-bacterial.
- Can be designed and manufactured into a specific shape.
- Sinks can be integrated.
- Resistant to minor staining.

Zinc
- Good heat conductor.
- Can be designed and manufactured to a desired shape.
- Sinks, drain boards, and trivets can be integrated.

Pewter
- Less clinical looking than stainless steel.
- Easily shaped and stamped for interesting designs.

What To Be Aware Of

Stainless Steel
• Shows fingerprints and scratches; texturing can help hide them.
• Can be visually cold; industrial feeling.
• Can warp if the gauge isn't heavy enough.
• May change color over time; a sealer or wax can help to retain the original finish.

Copper
• A periodic coat of butcher's or bee's wax is recommended.
• Scratches easily.
• Sharp implements can scratch the sealer, negating the benefits.

Zinc
• Susceptible to scratching; light scratching can be polished out.
• May distort if very hot items are placed on it.
• Avoid cutting or chopping on the surface.

Pewter
• Dents if struck hard enough.
• Very soft; susceptible to wear and tear.
• It is better suited as a secondary countertop.

Care | Cost

Care
Stainless Steel
• Use a stainless steel cleaner and soft cloth for general cleaning and to keep it shiny.
• Be careful with bleach and chlorine-based cleansers as they may permanently damage the surface.

Copper
• Clean with a soft rag and mild dish soap, dry with a clean cloth to prevent streaking.
• It can be polished with a commercial metal polish or some natural homemade methods.

Zinc
• Use a soft rag and mild dish soap for everyday cleaning.
• Apply beeswax for a deep luster.

Pewter
• Wipe up spills immediately and clean with warm water and mild dish soap.

Average Cost
• $75 and up per square foot, installed.

A pewter countertop crowns this elegant, regal bar. The 3 ½" countertop features a Verona edge detail. *Courtesy of Pewter by Design.*

The heavily detailed edge of this pewter countertop stands up to and reinforces the majesty of the carved corbel supports. *Courtesy of Pewter by Design.*

▲▶A coffee center is made topnotch with a 3 ¼" pewter countertop with a Cordoba edge detail. *Courtesy of Pewter by Design.*

◀▼A 3 ¼" Roma edged pewter countertop with a custom texture and patina pair beautifully with the blue island. *Courtesy of Pewter by Design.*

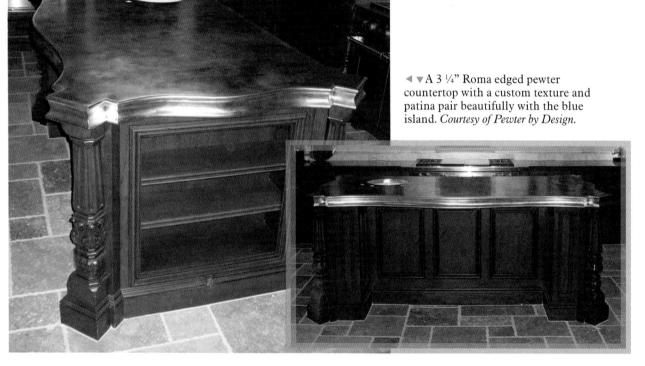

◀An antique Spanish cabinet paired with a pewter countertop is the ultimate in luxury repurposing. If you're looking for a statement piece for your kitchen or bar area, consider topping a piece of your heirloom – or hand-me-down – furniture with a countertop. *Courtesy of Pewter by Design.*

▲ A stainless steel countertop can work in a traditional, contemporary or country design. It offers great durability and aesthetics. *Courtesy of Handcrafted Metal.*

▲ A rope design on the apron of this zinc countertop would integrate beautifully into a kitchen with heavily carved cabinetry and millwork. *Courtesy of Handcrafted Metal.*

▲ A Mont Saint-Michel style edge works equally well in a traditional design as it does in a sleek and linear contemporary design. *Courtesy of Handcrafted Metal.*

▲ This zinc countertop sports a nouveau style curved front edge with squared edges. *Courtesy of Handcrafted Metal.*

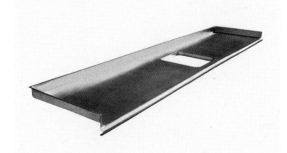

▲ A bullnose edge profile is commonly used with many countertop materials. The roundness of the bullnose is continued in the transition from countertop to backsplash on this zinc countertop. *Courtesy of Handcrafted Metal.*

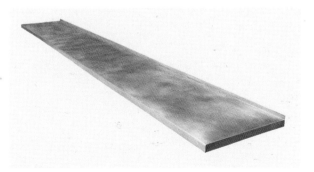

▲ This zinc countertop features squared corners and a small backsplash. It is shown with a medium patina. *Courtesy of Handcrafted Metal.*

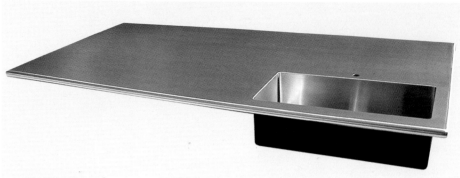

▲Pewter countertops can be fabricated with various edge profiles and designs. A very detailed edge profile can take a solid field countertop to a new level. Shown is the 2 ¼" Orleans edge detail. *Courtesy of Pewter by Design.*

▲A simple stainless steel countertop can be very elegant in a sophisticated design. *Courtesy of Handcrafted Metal.*

▲A free-form wavy backsplash adds a whimsical touch to this bullnose countertop. This custom piece was designed by the client. The butterfly finish on the backsplash is a nice complement to the jitterbug finish on the deck. Notice the play of light and reflection in the deck. *Courtesy of Handcrafted Metal.*

▲The Jardin de Giverny edge style features two indents, a rolled top edge, and dentil detail. This zinc countertop is fitted with a simple round hole to accept a round drop-in sink. *Courtesy of Handcrafted Metal.*

▲A hammered zinc countertop paired with white enameled cabinetry will keep the look simple yet elegant. *Courtesy of Handcrafted Metal.*

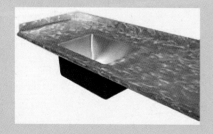

◀▶Do you want the light to dance and play across a countertop? Use a Butterfly finish. Here are examples of the finish on copper and stainless steel. *Courtesy of Handcrafted Metal.*

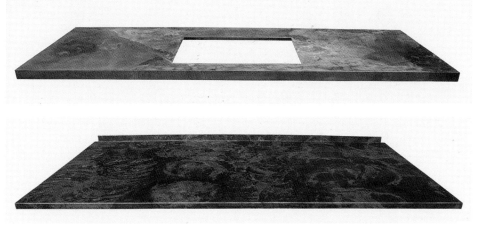

◄ ▲ Patinas on copper countertops, such as Crimson Sunset or Flame Swirl, add character and personality – no two countertops will be alike. *Courtesy of Handcrafted Metal.*

◄ This practical countertop features a durable reverse hammered surface and a raised marine edge to keep spills from hitting the floor. The backsplash is coved for easy cleaning and also has an integrated sink. *Courtesy of Handcrafted Metal.*

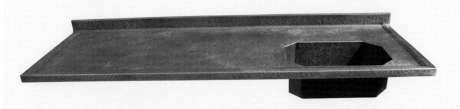

◄ A custom repoussed apron on an integrated sink can add a visual break from a smooth copper countertop without breaking the visual integrity of the material. *Courtesy of Handcrafted Metal.*

◄ A supremely simple countertop of copper. Consider copper when using a dark wood, such as wenge, for your cabinetry to create a design-forward dramatic effect. *Courtesy of Handcrafted Metal.*

◄ ▶ Add interest to your countertop's apron or corners with details of mixed metals or raised details such as clavos. *Courtesy of Handcrafted Metal.*

FROM

the look of rusting steel to intricately hand-painted designs, there is a ceramic tile to fit your style. They are available in mosaic and from 1 x 1" squares up to 24 x 28" rectangles with shiny or matte finishes. Highly detailed mosaics can be created from your design. Ceramic tile is suitable for contemporary or traditional settings. Coordinating tiles can be used as countertops, backsplashes, and flooring.

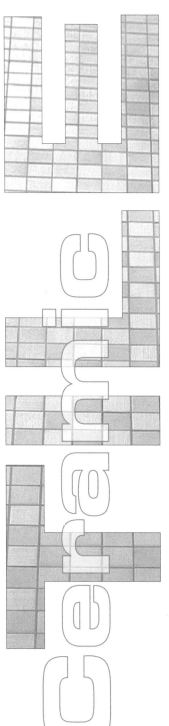

About the Material

Tile is primarily made of clay and various natural minerals and materials. The tile's strength comes from exposing the clay to extreme heat. Pigments can be added to the clay, creating a through-body tile, meaning that if it is chipped, the tile is the same color throughout. Ceramic tile is extremely porous unless it is glazed. Glazing is applied and fired onto some tiles, creating an impervious material. Different tiles are manufactured for specific purposes, whether they are for flooring, walls, or countertops – indoors or out. Check with your dealer to make sure the tile you are choosing is rated for your purpose.

Tile is adhered to the sub-surface with an adhesive and grouted into place. Depending on your design, the grout lines can vary in width.

If tile is installed correctly, it will last a lifetime.

What's Good About It

- Glazed tiles don't stain.
- Heat and burn resistant; ideal around cook surfaces.
- Makes a good do-it-yourself project.
- Tile is anti-bacterial.
- Individual damaged tiles can be replaced.
- Very low maintenance; very easy clean up.
- Will last a lifetime when installed properly.

What To Be Aware Of

- Uneven surface.
- Grout is more susceptible to stains, mold and mildew; sealant is recommended. Note: Epoxy grout is less susceptible to staining.
- Improper underlayment can cause grout to loosen, causing tiles to break.
- Chipping and scratching can occur.
- Tough on glassware.
- Can break if a heavy object lands on it.

Care | Cost

Care
- Clean with mild soap and warm water.
- The grout may need special attention as it can mildew or stain if not sealed or made with epoxy.

Average Cost
- $20 to $100 per square foot, installed.

◄ Decorative tile borders and colorful listellos surrounding solid field tiles show your personality and style. Shown here is a combination of bubbly retro flowers and field tiles with a subtle relief of vertical stripes. *Courtesy of Tile of Spain and Pamesa Ceramica.*

▶ A solid field countertop continued on a backsplash provides the perfect foil for decorative tiles that personalize a space. *Courtesy of Ceramic Tile of Italy.*

◄ Large rectangular format tiles on the countertop counterbalance the smaller square tiles on the backsplash. The two-tile formats work together to add textural interest to a monochromatic contemporary kitchen. *Courtesy of Tile of Spain and Equipe Cerámicas.*

▲Ceramic tile is a great way to add color to a countertop. Tile is also a great way to carry a color scheme throughout the room by using the same tile in varying sizes and textures. *Courtesy of Tile of Spain and Glass Cerámica S.L.*

◄Ceramic tiles average 1/16 to 5/16" in thickness, however, accessory pieces help add substance and depth to a countertop. *Courtesy of Ceramic Tiles of Italy.*

▲Because of new manufacturing techniques, the characteristic grout lines between ceramic tiles can be minimized. *Courtesy of Ceramic Tiles of Italy.*

▲Ceramic tile countertops provide a sleek, durable surface. Styles, colors, and formats are available to meet just about any design requirement. *Courtesy of Ceramic Tiles of Italy.*

▶Achieve an 'artsy-techie' look with these barcode tiles – notice the barcode carries from the backsplash to the countertop. *Courtesy of Ceramic Tile of Italy.*

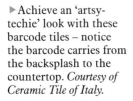

◄ Large format ceramic tiles meld well with a sleek, contemporary look. *Courtesy of Ceramic Tiles of Italy.*

▶ A white countertop and cabinetry boxes frame a beautiful wood door and drawer fronts. The white allows the wood's finish and graining to take center stage. *Courtesy of Ceramic Tiles of Italy.*

▶ Advanced coloring and pattern techniques allow ceramic tile to resemble natural stone. *Courtesy of Ceramic Tiles of Italy.*

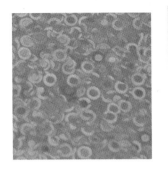

FROM

sleek colors to sophisticated stone looks to contemporary metal finishes to retro patterns, there are thousands of colors, textures, and patterns available in laminates. Laminates are easily combined with different edging materials like wood or metal for a custom design.

LAMINATE

About the Material

Laminate is made by binding layers of printed paper and resin under high pressure. This creates a rigid sheet that can be cut, shaped, and glued to a sub-surface such as MDF (medium density fiberboard). Because it is made with paper, anything can be printed on laminate, making it easy for companies to keep up with trends.

Some manufacturers use solid color plastic or melamine bases to retain surface color throughout. This makes scratches less noticeable and eliminates brown edges at joints.

What's Good About It

- Easy on the budget.
- Wide range of colors and styles.
- Easy to maintain.
- Can withstand years of use.
- An experienced do-it-yourselfer could install it.

What To Be Aware Of

- Susceptible to burns.
- Susceptible to scratches and chipping.
- Nearly impossible to repair, usually the entire surface has to be replaced.
- Moisture around edges and joints may dissolve glues and resins.
- Joints may be visible.

Care | Cost

- Use mild soap and water to remove most stains; try baking soda and water on tough stains.
- Avoid harsh abrasives, scrub pads, bleach, and ammonia to avoid discoloration.

Average cost
- $13 to $65 per sq. foot installed.

▶ The opulent mix of black and dark browns with warm brown pyrite-inspired highlights is enhanced by a natural wood edging. *Mineral Jet courtesy of Formica® Group.*

▶

◀ Texture, color variations, and an intricate edge profile in laminate can dress up otherwise simple cabinetry for a fraction of the cost of natural materials. *Courtesy of Wilsonart International, Inc.*

▲ ▶ Some laminate surfaces are inspired by the allure of natural minerals. Some collections include high-gloss, textured patterns with holographic facets that refract and reflect light. The countertop shown is rich with yellow, browns, and gold tones. *Radiance™ Mineral Ochre courtesy of Formica® Group.*

▲ Laminates nod to new-aged metallic influences. The deep brown laminate ▲ is accented with warm gold. *Bronze Rust courtesy of Formica® Group.*

◄ ▲ The timeless and beautiful look of wood is captured in this realistic polished wood grain in soft mellow hues of gold. *Planked Pear courtesy of this Formica® Group.*

▲ Advanced manufacturing techniques make interesting edge details possible for laminates. *Courtesy of Wilsonart International, Inc.*

◀▲The endless variety of available laminates can compliment a wide-range of kitchen styles. *Courtesy of Wilsonart International, Inc.*

◀Laminates that emulate gemstones and granites employ myriad color and texture to capture the look and feel of the natural material. *Raven Gemstone courtesy of Wilsonart International, Inc.*

◀Careful attention to subtle color variations in the manufacturing of laminates becomes dramatic when juxtaposed to a deep, rich wall color. *Jeweled Coral courtesy of Wilsonart International, Inc.*

▼Playful circles and complimentary colors play in this whimsical countertop. *Beluga courtesy of Formica® Group.*

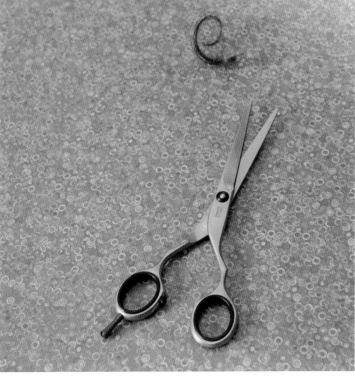

◀Just about any texture, color or material found in nature can be the inspiration for laminate. The laminate shown draws its character from seagrass. *Seagrass courtesy of Formica® Group.*

The rich veining and mottled earthy tones of slate are captured in laminate. *Colorado Slate courtesy of Formica® Group.*

◄Capture the nostalgia of days past with laminate. *Boomerang courtesy of Formica® Group.*

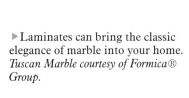

►Laminates can bring the classic elegance of marble into your home. *Tuscan Marble courtesy of Formica® Group.*

MYRIAD

colors and patterns – solids, speckled, metallic, gloss or matte – are available in solid surfacing. It can give the look of stone without the seams or color variations. When seams are necessary, they are typically inconspicuous. Fabrication techniques make unexpected contours easily formed for a unique design.

SOLID SURFACE

About the Material

Solid surface is a hard, dense material made from a mix of polyester and/or acrylic resins, fillers, and color pigments that are poured into molds. The color and pattern is consistent throughout the depth of the material. It is easily fabricated to meet the customer's specifications. Solid surface countertops are usually .5" to .75" thick. Backsplashes, sinks, and other special features can be integrated.

What's Good About It

- Virtually impossible to stain.
- Extremely durable; good for high use areas.
- Easy maintenance and clean up.
- Color won't fade.
- Surface is renewable because the color goes through the material.
- Burns, scratches, and chips can be sanded out and buffed back to a gloss.
- Dishware friendly.
- Sinks and special features can be integrated.
- Non-porous; hygienic and stain resistant.

What To Be Aware Of

- Looks less like natural stone.
- May crack after a hot item has been on it.
- Will stain or scratch; but they can be sanded out.

Care | Cost

Care
- Clean with warm, soapy water or an ammonia based cleaner and a clean cloth.
- The surface can be disinfected with a 1:1 solution of bleach and water.

Average Cost
- $40 to $100 per square foot, installed.

▲Warm lustrous copper tones draw the warmth of the wood▲
plank flooring up to eye level and help anchor the tall white
cabinetry in a room with high ceilings. *Copper Nugget courtesy of
Formica® Group.*

▶Small,
interesting cuts,
such as a sink
bump-out or
notches in an
island's corners,
help break up
the linearity
of long spans
of countertop.
*Courtesy of
Tempest by
Staron® Solid
Surfaces.*

▲ Solid surfaces offer consistency in color and pattern, ideal for large areas of countertop. *Courtesy of Tempest by Staron® Solid Surfaces.*

▼ Active work stations, like food preparation areas, benefit from the less porous nature of solid surfacing. *Courtesy of Tempest by Staron® Solid Surfaces.*

▲Tones of white cabinetry and countertop create a clean, yet stylish look. *Courtesy of Swanstone®.*

▲White countertops atop stained cabinetry set at different heights to accommodate various activities is practical and eye-appealing. *Courtesy of Swanstone®.*

▲The manufacturing techniques of solid surfacing easily lend themselves to unique shapes. *Courtesy of Swanstone®.*

▲ Specks of tone-on-tone hues throughout a solid surface countertop break the solid color of cabinetry without competing with the bold accent colors of the floor tile and stools. *Courtesy of Swanstone®.*

▲ Like many engineered surfaces, solid surfacing draws inspiration from nature. *Courtesy of Swanstone®.*

▲ The countertop mix in this kitchen creates an elegant yet rustic ambience. A solid surface material was used on the island with laminate topping the wall cabinetry. *Desert Mist solid surface and Mineral Ochre laminate courtesy of Formica® Group.*

◄ Different tones and colors of solid surfacing can be combined to create a unique countertop that reflects your style. *Courtesy of Mystera® Solid Surface.*

▶The ambience of fine imported stone can be captured in solid surfacing while offering a high level of hygienic properties. *Courtesy of Mystera® Solid Surface.*

▶Solid surfacing can be a cost effective alternative to natural stone. *Courtesy of Mystera® Solid Surface.*

▶Because the pattern, design, and color goes throughout a solid surface material, intricate edge patterns can be produced. *Courtesy of Mystera® Solid Surface.*

▲The edge detail of the higher island countertop ties the island and perimeter countertops together by combining their two materials. This is easily done with solid surface. *Courtesy of Mystera® Solid Surface.*

▼▶An accent color is added to the perimeter of the island countertop to create visual definition. *Courtesy of Mystera® Solid Surface.*

▲ Special features are easily incorporated into solid surfacing. Here, trivet rods ▲
are inlaid for the cook's convenience. *Courtesy of Mystera® Solid Surface.*

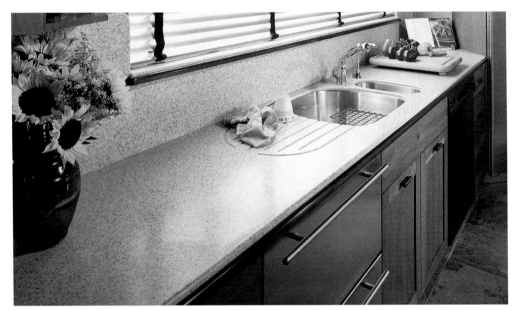

▶ Solid surfacing materials can be
used as backsplashes as well. Note
the drain runnels carved into the
surface by the sink. *Courtesy of
Staron® Solid Surfaces.*

▶ Concrete is the inspiration
for this solid surface. *Courtesy of
Formica® Group.*

◄ Solid surfacing can come in various thicknesses to create unique countertop looks. Shown is a 3-centimeter thick option. *Ivory Coast Quartz by InDepth Surfacing® courtesy of Formica® Group.*
◄

◄ The continuous field of solid surfacing plays well with the grout grids of tile. *Courtesy of Mystera® Solid Surface*

▲When a design calls for a classic natural marble feel but requirements don't allow for a natural material, solid surfacing may be able to provide the desired look. *Courtesy of Mystera® Solid Surface*

▶The myriad choices in solid surfaces make it one of the most design flexible materials on the market. *Courtesy of Mystera® Solid Surface*

▼With some solid surfacing materials, it is difficult to distinguish from a natural stone. *Courtesy of Mystera® Solid Surface*

▲ ▶ Solid surfacing inspired by the aesthetics of natural slate. *Courtesy of Mystera ® Solid Surface.*

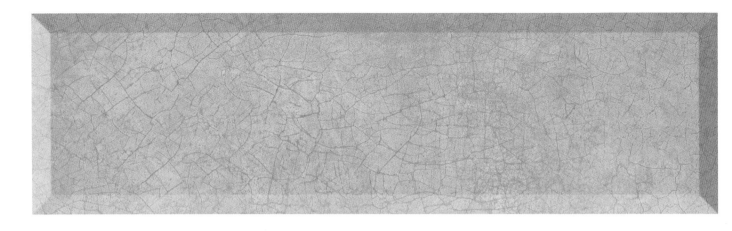

THE EDGE

profile on a countertop can transform any material into a desired look. In fact, the same material with different edge profiles can look completely different.

Contemporary or casual designs may require simple profiles, while intricate and detailed profiles may work better with more traditional designs. But, consider juxtaposing simple with ornate – the resulting look may be surprising.

This picture dictionary is just a sampling of possible edge profiles. Some manufacturers can design custom profiles.

Standard Roman

Profiles courtesy of The Grothouse Lumber Company and Innovative Stone.

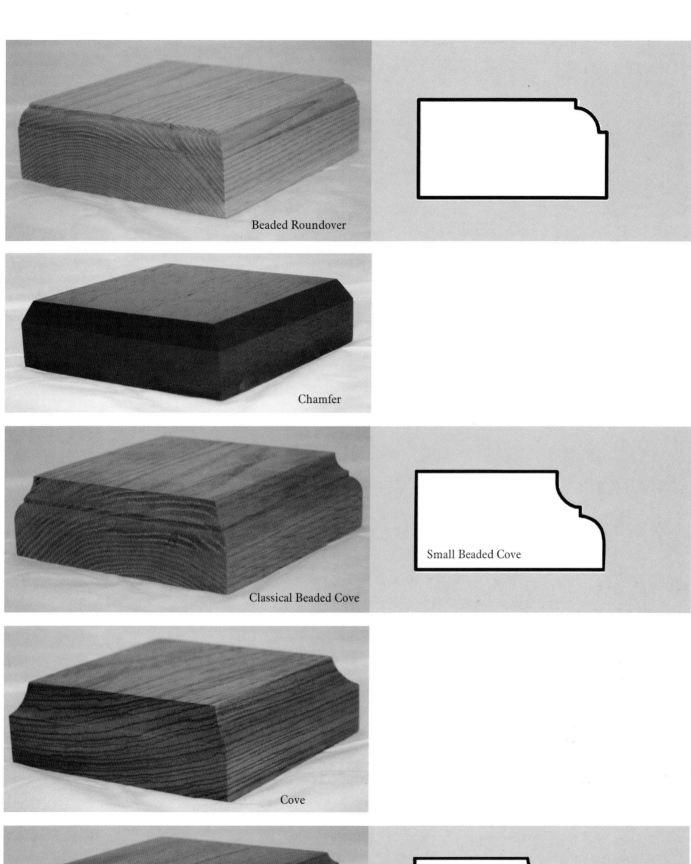

Beaded Roundover

Chamfer

Classical Beaded Cove

Small Beaded Cove

Cove

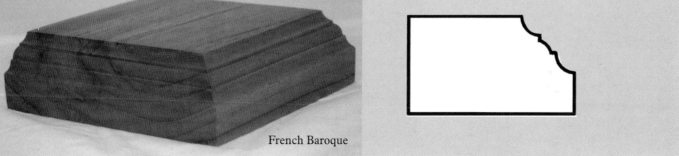

French Baroque

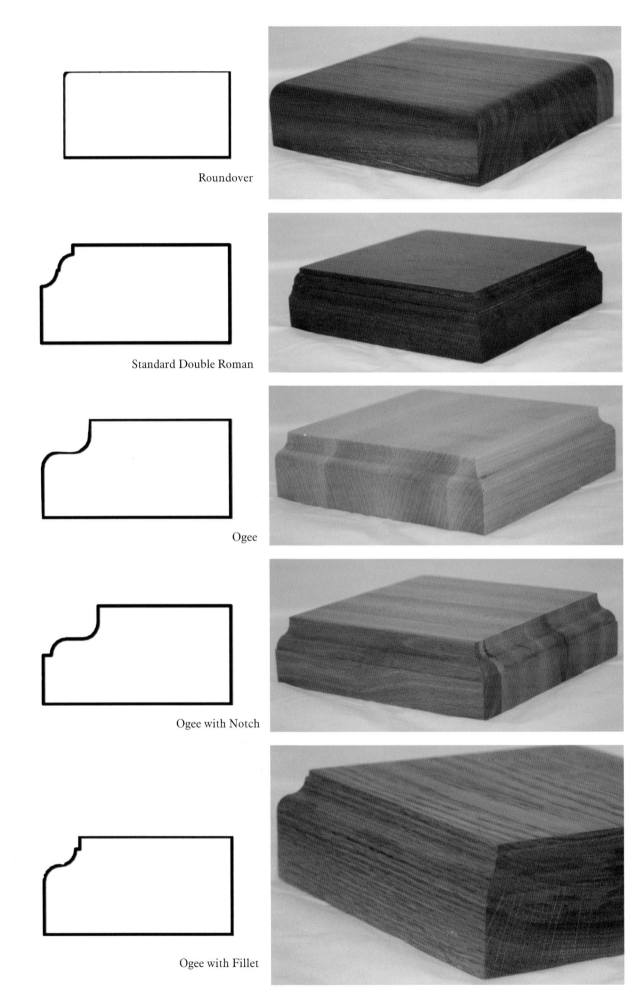

Roundover

Standard Double Roman

Ogee

Ogee with Notch

Ogee with Fillet

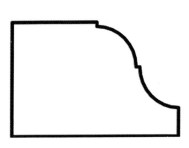

Cove Double Roman Ogee

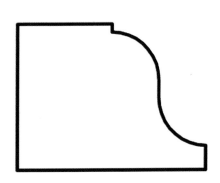

Medium Roman Ogee

Large Classical Beaded Cove

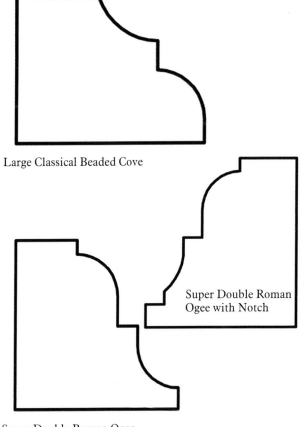

Super Double Roman Ogee with Notch

Super Double Roman Ogee

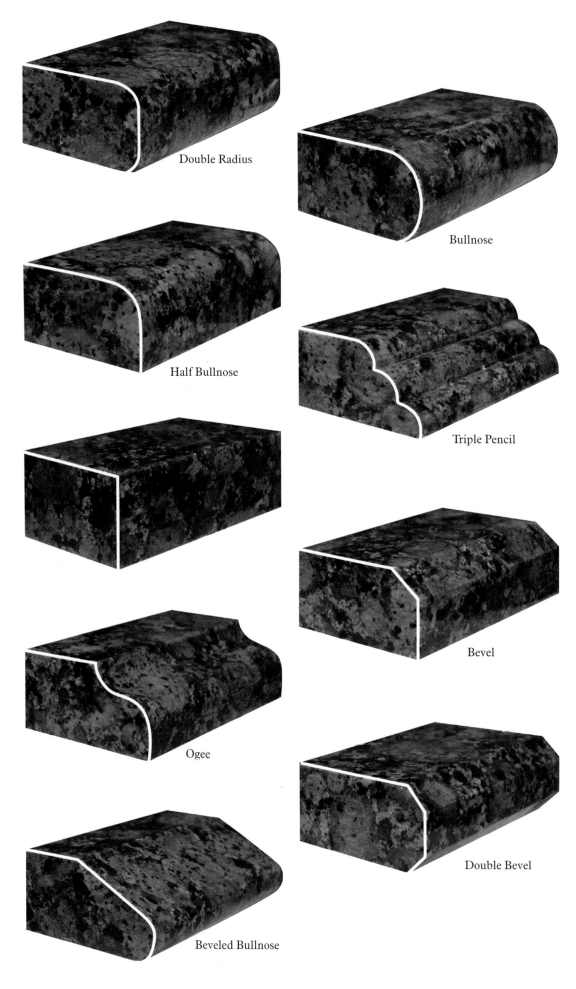

Double Radius

Bullnose

Half Bullnose

Triple Pencil

Ogee

Bevel

Double Bevel

Beveled Bullnose

CaesarStone USA
6840 Hayvenhurst Avenue, Suite 100
Van Nuys, CA 91406
1-877-9QUARTZ (978-2789)
1-818-779-0999
www.caesarstoneus.com
info@caesarstoneus.com

Cambria
11000 West 78th Street
Eden Praire, MN 55344
1-866-CAMBRIA (226-2742)
www.cambriausa.com

Draper-DBS™, Inc.
1803 North Fifth Street
Perkasie, PA 18944
(215) 257-3833
www.draperdbs.com
info@draperdbs.com

EnviroGlas
7704 San Jacinto Place, Suite 200
Plano, TX 75024
(972) 608-3790
www.enviroglasproducts.com
communications@enviroglasproducts.com

Equipe Cerámicas, S.L.
Ctra, CV-190, Km.9,1
Figueroles, Castellon, 12122
+34 964 38 19 07
www.equipeceramicas.com

Flying Turtle Cast Concrete
1314 Coldwell Avenue
Modesto, CA 95350
1-888-342-5100
(209) 530-1611
www.flyingturtlecastconcrete.com
sales@flyingturtle.us

Formica
1-800-FORMICA
www.formica.com

GerrityStone™
225B Merrimac Street
Woburn, MA 01801
(781) 938-1820
www.gerritystone.com

Glass Cerámicas, S.L.
Ctra. Puerto Viver-Burriana, Km. 55
Onda, Castellon, 12200
+34 964 38 19 00
+34 964 38 17 17
www.glassceramica.es

Green Mountain Soapstone Corp.
680 East Hubbardton Road
P.O. Box 807
Castleton, VT 05735
(802) 468-5636
www.greenmountainsoapstone.com
info@greenmountainsoapstone.com

The Grothouse Lumber Company
6035 Memorial Road
Germansville, PA 18053
1-877-268-5412
(610) 767-6515
www.glumber.com
glumber@glumber.com

Handcrafted Metal, Inc.
5121 E. 7th Street
Austin, TX 78702
1-800-755-0310
www.handcraftedmetal.com
sales@handcraftedmetal.com

Innovative Stone
Everlife™
150 Motor Parkway, Suite 210
Hauppauge, NY 11788
1-800-62STONE
www.innovativestone.com
www.everlifestone.com

Keeler Concrete Studio, Inc.
1721 S. West Street
Wichita, KS 67213
(316) 390-6733
www.keelerconcretestudio.com
jameskeeler9@yahoo.com

Majestic Gemstone
1-866-796-4939
www.majestic-gemstone.com
majesticgemstone@gmail.com

Mystera® Solid Surface
1-877-697-8372
www.mysterasurfaces.com

Pamesa Ceramica, S.L.
Camino Alcora, 8
Almazora, Castellon, 12550
+34 964 50 75 00
+34 964 52 27 16
www.pamesa.com

Pewter by Design
(415) 672-9555
www.pewterbydesign.com

Pyrolave® USA/J. Pauwels LLC
213 Fayetteville St. #200
Raleigh, NC 27601
(919) 788-8953
www.pyrolave.com
pyrolave@aol.com

Richlite Company
624 E. 15th Street
Tacoma, WA 98421
www.richlite.com
info@richlite.com

RMG Stone Products, Inc.
680 East Hubbardton Road
P.O. Box 807
Castleton, VT 05735
(802) 468-5636
www.rmgstone.com
rich@rmgstone.com

ShetkaStone L.L.C.
435 W Industrial Street
P.O. Box 38
Le Center, MN 56057
(507) 357-4177
www.shetkastone.com

Sonoma Cast Stone
1-877-283-2400
www.sonomastone.com

Staron
Samsung Chemical USA, Inc.
14251 E. Firestone Boulevard
La Mirada, CA 90638
1-800-795-7177
www.staron.com

Swanstone
The Swan Corporation
515 Olive Street, Suite 1800
St. Louis, Missouri 63101
1-800-325-7008
www.swanstone.com
infomail@swanstone.com

ThinkGlass
1993 Lionel-Bertrand
Boisbriand (Qc) Canada, J7H1N8
1-877-410-GLASS
(450) 420-1110
www.thinkglass.com

Tile of Spain
Trade Commission of Spain
2655 Le Jeune Road, Suite 1114
Coral Gables, FL 33134
(305) 446-4387
www.spaintiles.info

Trestlewood
P.O. Bo 1050
Pleasant Grove, UT 84062
1-877-375-2779
www.trestlewood.com
jsc@trestlewood.com

Trueform Concrete, LLC
5 Astro Place
Rockaway, NJ 07866
(973) 983-7500
www.trueformconcrete.com
info@trueformconcrete.com

UltraGlas®
9200 Gazette Avenue
Chatsworth, CA 91311
1-800-777-2332
www.ultraglas.com

UroGlass®
1611 Genessee, Suite 100
Kansas City, MO 64102
(816) 283-3876
www.uroglass.com
sales@uroglass.com

Vetrazzo
Ford Point, Suite 1400
1414 Harbour Way South
Richmond, CA 94804
(510) 234-5550
www.vetrazzo.com

Wilsonart International, Inc.
2400 Wilson Place
PO Box 6110
Temple, TX 76503-6110
1-800-433-3222
www.wilsonart.com
smartline@wilsonart.com

Xylem
470 Cloverleaf Drive, Unit C
Baldwin Park, CA 91706
1535 Oak Industrial Lane, Suite K
Cumming, GA 30041
1-866-395-8112
www.xylem.biz
info@xylem.biz

Joel Puliatti
Photographer for Vetrazzo
puliattiphoto@yahoo.com